GEOGRAPHY OF THE WORLD

SOUTH AMERICA

By Myra Weatherly

THE CHILD'S WORLD®
CHANHASSEN, MINNESOTA

Published in the United States of America by The Child's World®
P.O. Box 326, Chanhassen, MN 55317-0326
800-599-READ
www.childsworld.com

Photo Credits: Cover: Galen Rowell/Corbis; Animals Animals: 11(Mago-World Image), 17 (Lynn Stone), 20 (Mark Jones), 21 (Fabio Colombini Medeiros), 27 (Michael Reed); Corbis: 6 (Owen Franken), 8, 9 (Carl & Ann Purcell), 13 (Danny Lehman), 16 (Ludovic Maisant), 18 (Kevin Schafer), 23 (Jose Fuste Raga), 24 (Buddy Mays); Travelsite/Colosanti/Picture Desk: 7.

The Child's World®: Mary Berendes, Publishing Director
Editorial Directions, Inc.: E. Russell Primm, Editorial Director; Pam Rosenberg, Line Editor; Katie Marsico, Assistant Editor; Olivia Nellums, Editorial Assistant; Susan Hindman, Copy Editor; Elizabeth K. Martin, Proofreader; Ann Grau Duvall, Peter Garnham, Carol Yehling, Fact Checkers; Dr. Charles Maynara, Professor of Geography, Radford University, Radford, Virginia, Subject Consultant; Tim Griffin/IndexServ, Indexer; Cian Loughlin O'Day, Photo Researcher; Elizabeth K. Martin, Photo Selector; XNR Productions, Inc., Cartographer

Library of Congress Cataloging-in-Publication Data
Weatherly, Myra.
South America / by Myra Weatherly.
p. cm. — (Geography of the world series)
Includes bibliographical references and index.
ISBN 1-59296-062-6 (library bound : alk. paper)
1. South America—Juvenile literature. 2. South America—Geography—Juvenile literature. I. Title. II. Series.
F2208.5.W43 2004
980—dc21 2003006487

Table of Contents

CHAPTER ONE

Where Is South America?

South America lies southeast of North America. It is connected to North America by a land bridge called the Isthmus of Panama. Its boundaries are the Caribbean Sea on the north, the Pacific Ocean on the west, and the Atlantic Ocean on the east. To the south, a waterway known as the Drake Passage separates South America from frozen Antarctica.

SPACE LIFTOFF

Since 1968, Kourou, French Guiana (belonging to France) has been the site of the rocket launching pad of the European Space Agency. Its location near the equator makes French Guiana a better site than anyplace in Europe. Earth spins faster at the equator than anywhere else, so rockets receive an extra lift.

The **continent** lies completely in the Western **Hemisphere** between 81° west **longitude** and 35° west longitude. It stretches from 12° north **latitude** to 56° south latitude. Much of the land lies in the **Tropics.** The **equator** passes

A physical map of South America

through Ecuador, Colombia, and Brazil. There, steamy, hot weather is accompanied by heavy rainfall. Farther to the south is a subtropical region with cooler temperatures and less constant rainfall. The climate

DESTRUCTION OF THE AMAZON RAIN FOREST

In recent years, about 10 percent of the Amazon rain forest has been destroyed. Frequent earthquakes, volcanic eruptions, and fires cause damage. Clearing the forest to sell wood or to create new farms and developments further harms the forest. It also displaces the people and animals that live in the rain forest.

is much drier in central and southern South America. The far south experiences cold weather, with snow in the winter. The mountain regions have a wide range of temperatures and **precipitation,** depending on their **altitude.**

The Amazon River provides food and a means of transportation for the people who live in the rain forest.

The range of different landscapes in Chile makes it a country where farmlands, mountains, and coasts overlap.

About half of the continent's land is covered by forest. In the cooler and drier areas, prairie grasslands take over. About one-fourth of the land is used for grazing animals. Only 7 percent of the land is used for growing crops, such as corn, wheat, and rice.

The seasons south of the equator are the reverse of the seasons north of the equator. Because of this, in most of South America, January is in the middle of summer and July is a winter month.

CHAPTER TWO

How Did South America Come to Be?

About 250 million years ago, Earth was a very different place. Scientists believe that all of the present continents were clustered into one supercontinent surrounded by one gigantic ocean.

Scientists think the coast of Brazil (above) broke off from the western coast of Africa millions of years ago.

About 200 million years ago, the huge landmass, known as Pangaea, began to break up. Movement under the Earth's surface split Pangaea into smaller pieces of land. Over time, the two large pieces of Earth's crust split into more pieces. Then, these pieces separated and began to drift slowly into their present positions. Scientists have developed the theory of plate tectonics to explain this movement of the pieces of Earth's crust.

Many scientists believe that the coast of Rio de Janeiro was once in the middle of a large continent made up of present-day Africa and South America.

Scientists think that violent activity under the Earth's surface ripped South America from Africa. This belief is based on the geographic "fit" of the bulge of eastern South America and the western coast of Africa. After the split, the continent of South America began to drift westward. It is still on the move today.

HOME OF THE GIANT TORTOISE

The Galápagos Islands, located 650 miles (1050 km) off the coast of Ecuador, are famous for their unusual plant and animal life. The island chain bears the name of the giant Galápagos tortoise—now an endangered animal.

South America is the fourth largest of the world's seven continents. It covers an area of 6,885,000 square miles (17,833,000 square kilometers). The total area makes up about 12 percent of Earth's land surface.

The Andean Region includes the northern Andes Mountains and the surrounding areas of rain forests, grasslands, and deserts. As mountains go, the Andes are very young. They were thrust up from Earth's crust about 70 million years ago. Five of the continent's 12 nations—Venezuela, Colombia, Ecuador, Peru, and Bolivia—share this northwest region.

Brazil covers nearly half the land surface of South America. Here, both the Brazilian Plateau and Guiana Highlands are made of hard rock much older than the Andes.

The mountains of the beautiful Patagonian region in Chile are dotted with freshwater lakes.

THE MIGHTY AMAZON

The Amazon River begins high in the Peruvian Andes. It winds 4,000 miles (6,437 km) through the Brazilian rain forest to the Atlantic Ocean. Only the Nile River in Africa is longer.

Chile and Argentina are the two largest countries in the long, thin southern portion of South America. The landscape in Chile is dominated by the Andes Mountains. Argentina is known for its huge, grassy plain known as the Pampas.

CHAPTER THREE

What Makes South America Special?

The astounding natural wonders of South America lure visitors to the continent. From the snow-capped mountains to the driest deserts and stunning waterfalls, there is something for everyone.

The Andes Mountains form the longest mountain chain in the world. The narrow chain stretches more than 4,500 miles (7,421 km) along the entire west coast of South America. Only the Himalayas in Asia have higher mountains than the Andes. The highest peak in the Western Hemisphere is Argentina's Aconcagua. It soars 22,831 feet (6,961 meters) high. The breathtaking views from the high ridges of the Andes attract sightseers and mountain climbers.

Machu Picchu is South America's main tourist attraction. More than 300,000 people a year trek to the site. They marvel at the 500-year-old ruins of the once-proud Inca city high in the Peruvian Andes. The natives carved huge blocks of stone from the mountainsides to build their temples, palaces, and other structures. How they did this without knowing about the wheel baffles engineers. **Archeologists** believe that Machu Picchu was abandoned soon after the Spanish invasion in the 1500s.

The ruins of Machu Picchu were once the center of the Inca empire which ruled over the Andean region of South America before the Spanish conquistadors.

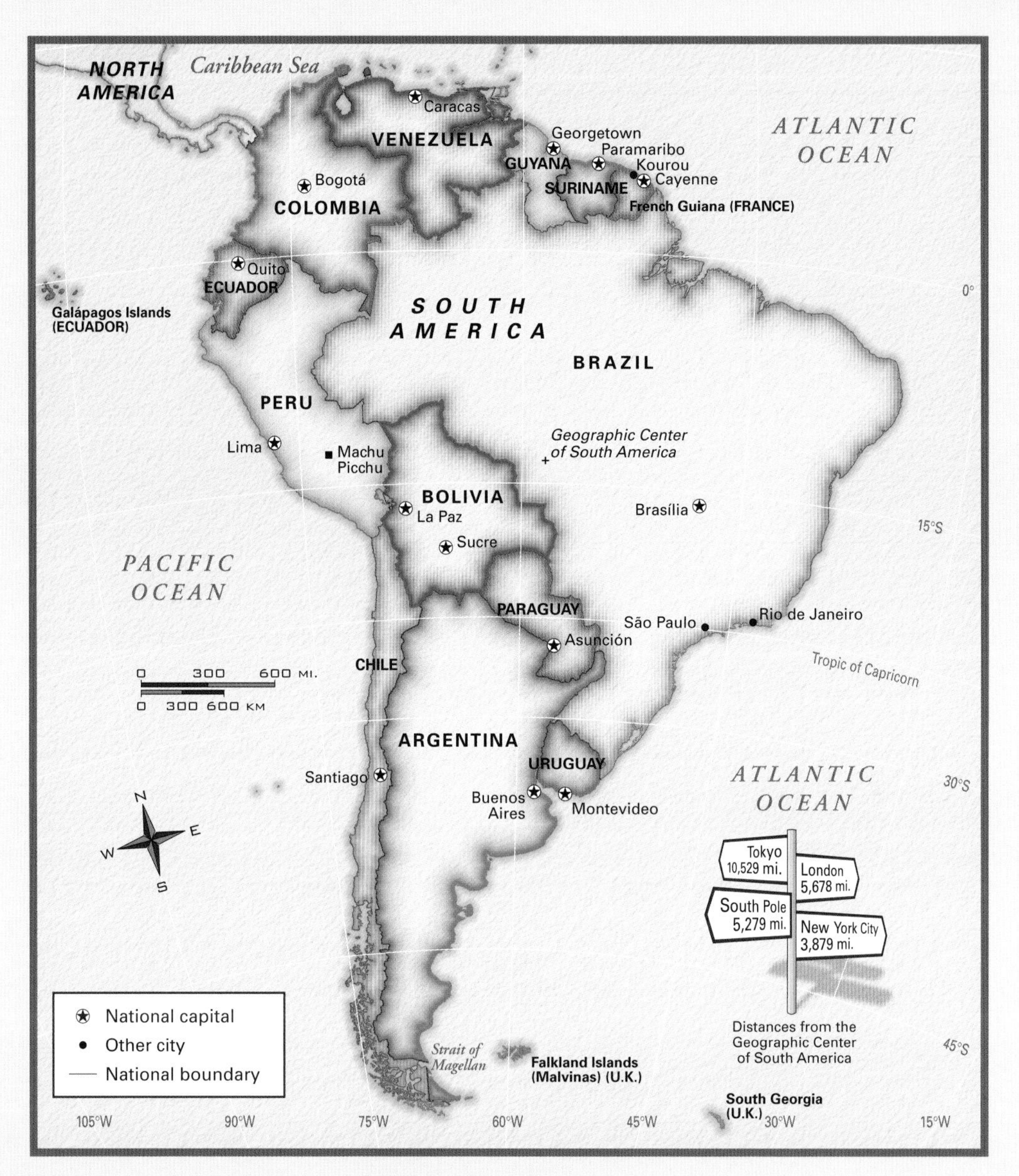

A political map of South America

For nature lovers, birdwatchers, and orchid fanciers, the Amazon rain forest is a natural paradise. An Amazon River cruise provides a good way to explore the rain forest. The Manu Biosphere Reserve—one of 17 **World Heritage Sites** on the continent—is one of the best areas for seeing wildlife. There is an abundance of monkeys (13 **species**), turtles, otters, tapirs, and jaguars. The rich bird life includes macaws, toucans, and curassows.

STEAMING CRATER

Cotopaxi in Ecuador is the highest active volcano in the world. After reaching the top, an anthropologist wrote: "From the icebound rim of Cotopaxi's steaming crater at 19,347 feet (5,898 m), I could see 12 other snow peaks, most of them volcanoes, lifting out of meadows and rain forests."

Those seeking adventure will find it in the Atacama Desert. Spectacular landscapes and natural wonders abound. The desert runs along the coast of Chile for 2,000 miles (3,217 km). The Atacama Desert is the driest area on Earth. Some parts of the desert have not received rainfall in 400 years. Salt basins, sand, lava flows, and copper mines make up the Atacama. Mysterious gigantic drawings adorn the hillsides.

The Atacama Desert in Chile is the driest place on Earth.

A CHILLING DISCOVERY

In 1995, a climber in the Peruvian Andes discovered the mummified remains of a teenager. The "Ice Maiden" had been buried for 500 years before a snowslide dislodged her remains. Once the frozen mummy was safely down the mountain, scientists worked to preserve the body.

Patagonia, in southern Argentina, is also dry. With an area of about 260,000 square miles, (670,000 sq km), Patagonia forms the largest desert in the Americas. Today, the region's national parks and reserves attract many people. They also protect the vast array of plant and animal life. At Los Glaciers National Park, visitors can hear and see **glaciers** slowly grinding their way downhill before plunging into lake water.

CHAPTER FOUR

What Animals and Plants Are Found in South America?

The Amazon rain forest contains thousands of different species of animals and plants. The leading member of the Amazon wildlife community is the jaguar, the largest wildcat in the Americas. Jaguars can weigh up to 350 pounds (159 kilograms). They live by feeding on

A jaguar stalks his prey through the Costa Rican rain forest.

Woolly spider monkeys generally live in groups of 10 to 12, but they have been seen in groups as large as 70.

ANACONDA SNAKE

The anaconda is one of the world's largest snakes. These reptiles can grow as long as 30 feet (9 m) and weigh as much as 400 pounds (181 kg). The anaconda snake feeds on almost anything. It lurks beneath the surface of waters or slithers among tree branches, stalking its prey. When the perfect moment arrives, the anaconda strikes.

other animals, such as tapirs and giant otters. A jaguar pounces on its prey, quickly breaking the animal's neck with a powerful bite.

The Incas respected these beautiful, fierce cats. They used the jaguar's image on their coat of arms. Hunting and the destruction of forests threaten the jaguar's existence. Anaconda snakes are the jaguar's only natural predators.

Many kinds of monkeys, including the wooly spider monkey, swing through the treetops of the rain forest. Beautiful birds, such as toucans, parrots, and macaws, live in the forest. Many other species of birds make their home in the jungle, too.

The rain forest of South America contains more species of plants than any other region in the world. There are more than 2,500 kinds of trees. Many useful products come from the green tangle of rain forest plants. Dozens of species of plants are used in medicines for fighting malaria, coughs, and infections. Tropical forests are also a source for industrial products such as rubber.

Compared with the forests, South America's pampas (grasslands) have fewer plants and animals. Among the animals found here are the ocelot, puma, armadillo, wolf, bush dog, and the giant anteater. The largest rodent is the capybara. Some capybaras weigh more than

Llamas are used as pack animals by people who live in the Andes Mountains.

ANDEAN CONDOR

The Andean condor lives in the Andes Mountains. These huge birds have a wingspan of about 10 feet (3 m). They soar among the steep cliffs and look for the remains of dead animals on which to feed.

150 pounds (68 kg). The best-known bird in this region is the flightless, ostrich-like rhea.

The surefooted llama, guanaco, and vicuña—all relatives of the camel—live in the mountains of South America. They are used as pack animals in the high Andes and are also prized for their fine wool. The spectacled bear and mountain lion, as well as the giant toad and Andean iguana, make their homes in the mountains. The tall trees of the Andes Mountains supply many birds, such as the condor and the flicker, with homes. Scattered cactuses and small shrubs grow on the slopes of the Andes.

Animals found in the harsh deserts of South America include llamas, armadillos, foxes, hawks, and eagles. Flamingoes inhabit the areas in and around the salt lakes. Of all the animals found in the deserts, insects are the most numerous. Some kinds of plants have adapted to the extreme dryness of the Atacama Desert by developing roots that run deep into the ground. These tap roots allow the plant to use water far below the surface of the desert. These plants are important for the survival of desert animals and insects. There is almost no plant life in the interior of the desert.

The hairy armadillo can roll into a ball to protect itself from predators.

CHAPTER FIVE

WHO LIVES IN SOUTH AMERICA?

Asiatic hunters and gatherers were probably the first settlers in South America. It is believed that they arrived about 11,000 years ago—and possibly much earlier. When the Spanish arrived from Europe in the 1500s, they found a thriving civilization—the huge Inca empire. The Spanish invaders stole the riches of the Incas and destroyed their mighty empire. By the end of the 1500s, Portugal claimed Brazil, while Spain controlled the rest of the continent. Much later, people from other European countries settled in South America.

SPANISH CONQUEROR

Francisco Pizarro, with only a few men, invaded and defeated the Inca Empire in 1532. He ordered the killing of Incan ruler Atahualpa. After his victory, he claimed most of South America for Spain.

Several groups of people make up modern South America. The population includes native people, sometimes called

This statue of Francisco Pizarro commemorates his quick victory over the Inca empire.

Amerindians, and people of European and African descent. Many people are mestizos—people of mixed descent.

More than 20 million people live in the high Andes. The people who live at high altitudes have developed extra-large lungs to help them breathe better. They

YANOMAMI

Twenty thousand Yanomami live in huts deep inside the Amazon rain forest. They hunt with long arrows—just as their forefathers did. They wear little clothing, painting their bodies instead. In recent years, gold miners invaded. They brought sadness, destruction, and diseases. In 1992, the government of Brazil declared Yanomami land off-limits to outsiders.

A weekend market in the Peruvian Andes

are descendants of the Incas and other native people. They keep to their old ways and customs. The Andean people farm and raise livestock in the same way their ancestors did centuries ago.

Although native languages are still spoken in remote areas, most of the people of South America speak Spanish. People in Brazil speak Portuguese. The majority of the Amerindians are Quechua-speaking people.

Large parts of the continent have almost no people. Three out of four of South America's 323 million people live in cities. The most thickly populated are the continent's largest cities—São Paulo and Rio de Janeiro in Brazil, and Buenos Aires in Argentina.

CHAPTER SIX

What Is South America Like Today?

Compared to North America, Europe, and Asia, South America is a poor continent. It stands on the edge of becoming a major world power—but it has not yet become one. The people who govern South American countries must work to overcome the problems of their countries.

SOCCER

South America is soccer crazy. The popular sport is played throughout much of the continent. South American teams have claimed the World Cup eight times.

Today, millions of South Americans face terrible poverty, hunger, and disease. Shantytowns—places where people live in little more than old cardboard boxes—are packed with jobless people and can be found on the outskirts of major cities. Gangs of homeless children roam the streets. Their search for food often takes them to heaps of disease-infested garbage.

The illegal drug trade continues to be a problem in South America, especially in Colombia, Peru, and Bolivia. Thousands have died in the war on drugs.

South America's economy is based on agriculture, but less than half of the continent's farmable land is being used. Commercial crops—coffee, bananas, sugarcane, wheat, and cocoa beans—grow on large plantations. Most of the farming consists of growing basic food crops on small plots of land. Corn is the most widely grown food crop.

The grasslands of South America produce beef cattle and sheep. The livestock industry provides meat, leather goods, and wool for local people and overseas markets.

South America's plentiful supply of minerals includes iron ore, bauxite, petroleum, copper, tin, gold, silver, lead, diamonds, and emeralds. Unfortunately, mining the land for these minerals is often bad for

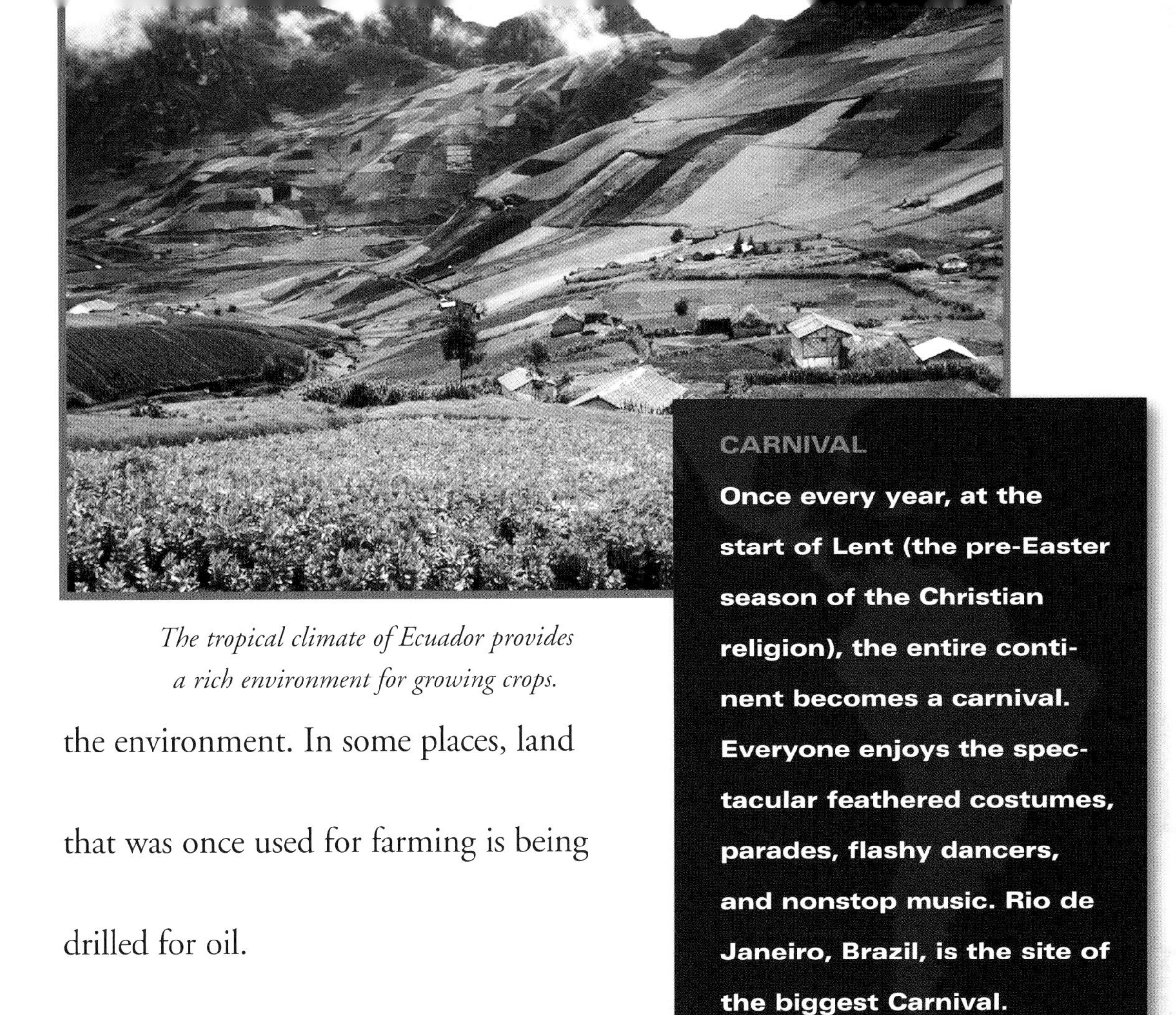

The tropical climate of Ecuador provides a rich environment for growing crops.

the environment. In some places, land that was once used for farming is being drilled for oil.

CARNIVAL

Once every year, at the start of Lent (the pre-Easter season of the Christian religion), the entire continent becomes a carnival. Everyone enjoys the spectacular feathered costumes, parades, flashy dancers, and nonstop music. Rio de Janeiro, Brazil, is the site of the biggest Carnival.

South America's future looks promising. However, people must find creative ways to solve problems such as the wide gap between rich and poor and the drug problem. They must also find ways to use their many resources without harming the environment. Then future generations will be able to enjoy the beauty of their South American continent.

Glossary

altitude (AL-ti-tood) Altitude is the height of an object above the ground.

archeologists (ar-kee-OL-uh-jists) Archeologists are scientists who dig up and study the material remains of past human life and activities, such as fossils, buildings, and objects.

continent (KON-tuh-nuhnt) A continent is one of the seven large landmasses on Earth.

equator (i-KWAY-tur) The equator is an imaginary line that circles Earth halfway between the North and South Poles.

glaciers (GLAY-shurs) Glaciers are huge sheets of ice.

hemisphere (HEM-uhss-fihr) One half of a sphere, such as the northern half or southern half of Earth when it is divided in two by the equator, is called a hemisphere.

latitude (LAT-uh-tood) Latitude is the position of a place on the globe as it is measured in degrees north or south of the equator.

longitude (LON-juh-tood) Longitude is the position of a place on the globe as it is measured in degrees east or west of an imaginary line known as the prime meridian. The prime meridian runs through the Greenwich Observatory in London, England, and is sometimes called the Greenwich Meridian.

precipitation (pri-sip-ih-TAY-shuhn) Water that falls from the sky in the form of rain, snow, sleet, or hail is called precipitation.

rain forest (RAYN FOR-ist) A rain forest is a tropical forest where a lot of rain falls.

species (SPEE-sheez) A species is a group of animals or plants that share a certain characteristics.

Tropics (TROP-iks) The Tropics is the area of the earth near the equator where temperatures are hot all year round.

World Heritage Sites (WURLD HER-uh-tij SITES) World Heritage Sites are places that have been designated as having great significance to the cultural and/or natural history of the world. The list of World Heritage Sites is created by the United Nations Educational, Scientific and Cultural Organization (UNESCO).

A South American Almanac

Location on the Globe:
Longitude: 81° west to 35° west
Latitude: 12° north to 56° south

Greatest distance from north to south: 4,750 miles (7,645 km)

Greatest distance from east to west: 3,200 miles (5,150 km)

Borders: Caribbean Sea, Atlantic Ocean, Drake Passage, Pacific Ocean, Panama

Total Area: 6,899,000 square miles (17,868,000 sq km)

Highest Point: Mount Aconcagua, 22,831 feet (6,961 m) above sea level

Lowest Point: Valdes Peninsula, 131 feet (40 m) below sea level

Number of Countries on the Continent: 12

Major Mountain Ranges: Andes, Brazilian Highlands, Guiana Highlands

Major Deserts: Atacama, Patagonia

Major Rivers: Amazon, Madeira, Magdalena, Orinoco, Paraguay, Parana, Pilcomayo, Purus, Sao Francisco, Uruguay

Major Lakes: Maracaibo, Mirim, Poopo, Titicaca

Major Cities:
São Paulo, Brazil
Buenos Aires, Argentina
Bogotá, Colombia
Rio de Janeiro, Brazil
Lima, Peru

Languages: Spanish, Portuguese, Dutch, English, Guarani, Quechua, Aymara

Population: 346,960,000 (estimated 2000)

Religions: Christianity (mainly Roman Catholicism), Judaism, Shamanism, Buddhism, Hinduism

Mineral Resources: Bauxite, coal, copper, emeralds, gold, iron ore, lead, manganese, petroleum, sodium nitrate, tin, zinc

South America in the News

1,000,000 B.C.	Ice covers the Andes Mountains in South America from Ecuador to Tierra del Fuego.
8,000 B.C.	The landscape of present-day South America begins to take shape as the glacial ice retreats.
900 – 200 B.C.	Chavín civilization flourishes in Peru.
1498	Christopher Columbus lands in present-day Venezuela.
1500	Pedro Alvares Cabral lands in present-day Brazil and claims it for Portugal.
1525	The first permanent Spanish settlement in South America is founded in present-day Colombia.
A.D. 1532	Spanish forces led by Francisco Pizarro conquer the Incan empire and claim Peru for Spain.
1537	Juan de Ayolas, a Spanish explorer, builds a fort at present-day Asuncion in Paraguay.
1580	Spanish settlers establish Buenos Aires in present-day Argentina.
1750	Portugal and Spain sign a treaty dividing South America between the two countries.
1783	Simón Bolívar is born in Caracas, Venezuela.
1811 – 1821	Venezuela, Peru, Colombia, Ecuador, Bolivia, and Argentina declare their independence from Spain.
1822	Brazil declares its independence from Portugal.
1864 – 1870	Argentina, Brazil, and Uruguay fight against Paraguay in the War of the Triple Alliance, or Paraguayan War. Paraguay is left in ruins.
1879 – 1883	Chile fights against Bolivia and Peru in the War of the Pacific.
1932 – 1935	The Chaco War is fought between Paraguay and Bolivia and Bolivia loses a large part of its territory to Paraguay.
1945	Eva Duarte marries Juan Perón. When Perón is elected president of Argentina in 1946, she becomes the most powerful woman in Argentina.
1985	Nevado del Ruiz, a volcano in the Andes mountains, erupts twice, triggering mudslides and floods, and claiming 25,000 lives.
1970	Salvador Allende Gossens is elected president of Chile, becoming the first democratically-elected Marxist to lead a country in the Western Hemisphere.
1999	Floods and mudslides triggered by heavy rains claim about 30,000 lives in Venezuela.

How to Learn More about South America

At the Library

Blue, Rose, and Corinne Naden. *Andes Mountains.* Austin, Tex.: Raintree Steck-Vaughn, 1995.

Pollard, Michael. *The Amazon.* New York: Marshall Cavendish, 1998.

Porter, Malcolm, and Keith Lye. *South America and Antarctica.* Austin, Tex.: Raintree Steck-Vaughn, 1999.

Reinhard, Johan. *Discovering the Inca Ice Maiden.* Washington, D.C.: National Geographic Society, 1998.

Savage, Stephen. *Animals of the Rain Forest.* Austin, Tex.: Raintree Steck-Vaughn, 1997.

Schwartz, David M. *Yanomami.* New York: Lothrop, Lee & Shepard, 1995.

On the Web

Visit our home page for lots of links about South America:

http://www.childsworld.com/links.html

Note to Parents, Teachers, and Librarians: We routinely verify our Web links to make sure they're safe, active sites—so encourage your readers to check them out!

Places to Visit or Contact

THE FIELD MUSEUM

To tour the museum's exhibit on plate tectonics

1400 South Lake Shore Drive

Chicago, IL 60605

312/922-9410

NATIONAL GEOGRAPHIC SOCIETY

To write for information about its many educational programs and publications

1145 17th Street N.W.

Washington, DC 20036-4688

800/647-5463

Index

About the Author

Myra Weatherly is the author of many books for children and young adults, including *Women Pirates: Eight Stories of Adventure, William Marshal: Medieval England's Greatest Knight, Dolley Madison: America's First Lady,* and *The Taj Mahal.* She has also written *Tennessee, South Carolina,* and *Nebraska* in the America the Beautiful series, as well as *The Thirteen Colonies: New Jersey.* In addition to her writing, Weatherly enjoys sharing her books with young people, traveling, and reading.